Wedding Planner Booklet

Annie L Watts

7121 Pacific Rim Highway

Port Alberni, BC

Canada, V9Y 8Y4

www.annielwatts.com

ISBN 978-1-365-82169-1 (paperback)

Planner Booklet

May your wedding day and honeymoon
runs smoothly.

First Edition, 2021
Annie L Watts

Table of Contents

Names and Telephone Numbers

Bride: _____

Groom: _____

Bridesmaids: _____

Groomsmen: _____

Flower girl: _____

Ring bearer: _____

Mother of the bride: _____

Mother of the groom: _____

Father of the bride: _____

Father of the groom: _____

Officiant: _____

Wedding Details

Engagement date: _____

Wedding date: _____

Bridal salon: _____

Hair stylist: _____

Make-up artist: _____

Men's attire store: _____

Wedding night accommodations: _____

Honeymoon travel agent: _____

Ceremony venue: _____

Reception venue: _____

Wedding photographer: _____

DJ or band: _____

Caters: _____

Bakery: _____

Liquor license: _____

Event insurance: _____

Printers: _____

Wedding Budget

Bachelorette party $ _____

Bachelor party $ _____

Engagement ring $ _____

Wedding ring $ _____

Wedding band $ _____

Bridal shower $ _____

Rehearsal dinner $ _____

Brides wedding gown $ _____

Bridesmaid's dresses $ _____

Grooms tuxedo $ _____

Groomsmen's suits $ _____

Flower girl dress $ _____

Ring bearer suit $ _____

Bouquets $ _____

Corsages $ _____

Ceremony venue $ _____

Reception venue $ _____

Photographer $ _____

Guest book $ _____

Wedding favors $ _____

Catering $ _____

Cake and cutting fee $ _____

Centerpieces $ _____

DJ or band $ _____

Honeymoon $ _____

Officiant fee $ _____

Limo rental $ _____

Wedding night $ _____

Total budget $_____

Wedding Ring

Bride's engagement and wedding ring size: _____

Groom's wedding band size: _____

Jewelers: _____

Address: _____

_____

Contact person: _____

Telephone number: _____

Bridal Gown

Style of bridal gown: _____

Size of bridal gown: _____

Bridal accessories: _____

Color of bridal party dresses: _____

Sizes of bridal party dresses: _____

Retailer: _____

Contact person: _____

Address: _____

_____

Telephone: _____

Groom's Suit

Style of groom's suit: _____

Color of groom's suit: _____

Size of groom's suit: _____

Groom's accessories: _____

Color of groomsmen's suits: _____

Sizes of groomsmen's suits: _____

Retailer: _____

Contact person: _____

Address: _____

_____

Telephone: _____

Wedding Flowers

Color scheme and type of flowers for the:

Bridal bouquet: _____

Bridesmaid's bouquets: _____

Corsages for the groom and groomsmen: _____

Flowers for the ceremony venue: _____

Centerpieces for the tables: _____

Florist: _____

Contact person: _____

Address: _____

_____

Telephone: _____

Wedding Cake

Flavors of the wedding cake: _____

Color scheme of the wedding cake: _____

Wedding cake delivery fee: _____

Wedding cake cutting and serving fee: _____

Baker: _____

Contact person: _____

Address: _____

_____

Telephone: _____

Wedding Photography

- ☐ Bride getting dressed
- ☐ Bride's dress
- ☐ Bride alone
- ☐ Bride with mom
- ☐ Bride with dad
- ☐ Bride with parents
- ☐ Bride with siblings
- ☐ Bride with parents and each set of grandparents
- ☐ Bride with immediate family and grandparents
- ☐ Bride with immediate family, no grandparents
- ☐ Bride with each attendant
- ☐ Bride with flower girl
- ☐ Bride with all attendants
- ☐ Seating of grandparents
- ☐ Bride and father preparing to walk down the aisle
- ☐ Attendants lined up for processional
- ☐ Musicians
- ☐ Groom waiting for bride
- ☐ Bride walking down the aisle
- ☐ Parents giving away the bride
- ☐ Bride and groom at the altar

- ☐ Bride and groom with bridesmaids and groomsmen
- ☐ Bride and groom exchanging vows
- ☐ Bride and groom exchanging rings
- ☐ Bride and groom's first kiss
- ☐ Bride and groom with officiant
- ☐ Bride and groom returning up the aisle
- ☐ Bride and groom with the bride's parents
- ☐ Bride and groom with the groom's parents
- ☐ Bride and groom romantic portraits
- ☐ Bride and groom at the receiving line
- ☐ Wedding party's entrance
- ☐ Bride and groom's entrance
- ☐ Bride and groom seated with wedding party
- ☐ Bride and groom's first dance
- ☐ Bride and bride's father dancing
- ☐ Groom and groom's mother dancing
- ☐ Bride and groom's father dancing
- ☐ Groom and bride's mother dancing
- ☐ Bride and groom cutting the wedding cake
- ☐ Bride and groom feeding wedding cake to each other
- ☐ Toasts
- ☐ Centerpieces
- ☐ Favors
- ☐ Bouquet toss
- ☐ Guests dancing
- ☐ Bride's parents dancing
- ☐ Groom's parents dancing
- ☐ Bride and groom in the limo
- ☐ Bride and groom waving goodbye to the guests

Wedding Guest List

Total Guest Count:

_____

_____
_____
_____
_____
_____
_____
_____
_____
_____
_____
_____
_____
_____
_____
_____
_____
_____
_____
_____
_____
_____
_____
_____
_____
_____

Wedding Timeline

Bride arrives at hair salon at 9 a.m.

Bride travels to the ceremony venue at 10:30 a.m.

Bridesmaids arrive at the ceremony venue to set up 11:00 a.m.

Bridesmaids start to get dressed 1:00 p.m.

Bridesmaids still picture photo op, 2:00 p.m.

Groomsmen still picture photo op, 2:30 p.m.

Wedding parties prepares for ceremony, 3:00 p.m.

Ceremony begins, 3:30 p.m.

Bride and groom ride limo to reception hall, 4:30 p.m.

Greet guests at reception hall, 5:00 p.m.

Introduce the bridal party, 5:30 p.m.

Toasts, 6:00 p.m.

Dinner served, 6:30 p.m.

Wedding cake cutting, 7:30 p.m.

Bouquet toss, 8:00 p.m.

Dancing, 8:30 p.m.

Everyone goes home at 11:30 p.m.

Dance Music

All of me, John Legend

2 become 1, Spice Girls

At last, Etta James

Love story, Taylor Swift

A thousand years, Christina Perri

Thinking out loud, Ed Sheeran

Can't help falling in love, Elvis

How long will I love you, Ellie Goulding

From this moment on, Shania Twain

Chapel of love, The Dixie Cups

Marry you, Bruno Mars

Ever ever after, Carry Underwood

You're still the one, Shania Twain

More than words, Extreme

Make you feel my love, ADELE

Stand by me, Ben E. King

Happy, Pharrell Williams

I will always love you, Whitney Houston

Because you loved me, Celine Dion

Kiss me, Sixpence Non The Richer

Packing List

- ☐ bridesmaid gifts
- ☐ groomsmen gifts
- ☐ marriage license
- ☐ passport
- ☐ cell phone and charger
- ☐ driver's license
- ☐ car keys
- ☐ wedding ring and band
- ☐ wedding dress
- ☐ bridal purse
- ☐ wedding jewelry
- ☐ wedding shoes
- ☐ wedding suit
- ☐ sash
- ☐ rehearsal dinner dress
- ☐ rehearsal suit
- ☐ rehearsal dinner shoes
- ☐ underwear and socks
- ☐ pajamas and housecoat
- ☐ slippers
- ☐ shampoo
- ☐ facewash
- ☐ body wash
- ☐ make-up
- ☐ moisturizer
- ☐ shaver and shaving cream
- ☐ toothbrush and floss
- ☐ hair brush
- ☐ hair spray and hair gel
- ☐ curling iron

Notes